Success Tweets

For Administrative Professionals

200 Bits of Common Sense Career Advice
For Administrative Professionals
All in 140 Characters or Less

BUD BILANICH
The Common Sense Guy

With

KETTY ORTEGA and
CHRISSY SCIVICQUE

FRONT ROW PRESS

Front Row Press
191 University Boulevard, #414 • Denver, CO 80206 • 303.393.0446

This book is for Cathy
xoxoxoxoxoxoxoxoxoxoxoxoxoxoxoxoxoxoxoxo
xoxoxoxoxoxoxoxoxoxoxoxoxoxoxoxoxoxoxoxo
xoxoxoxoxoxoxoxoxoxoxoxoxoxoxoxoxoxoxoxo
xoxoxoxoxoxoxoxoxoxoxoxoxoxoxoxoxoxoxoxo
xoxoxoxoxoxoxoxoxoxoxoxoxoxoxoxoxoxoxoxo
xoxoxoxoxoxoxoxoxoxoxoxoxoxoxoxoxoxoxoxo
xoxoxoxoxoxoxoxoxoxoxoxoxoxoxoxoxoxoxoxo

That's 140 hugs and kisses…

Thanks for your love and support.

Introduction

This is a success book, done in tweet format. It's a real book that will help you create the successful Administrative Professional career you want and deserve.

It gives you 200 pieces of common sense career success advice, all in 140 characters or less.

It will tell you how to succeed in your Administrative Professional career, 1 tweet at a time. You'll get the essentials with no fluff.

From now on "AP" will be used instead of the words "Administrative Professional." This saves space. Tweets can be 140 characters only.

Creating the successful AP career you deserve should be fun and exciting. This book will show you how.

Your time is valuable. You don't want to waste it. That's why you get 200 pieces of AP career advice all in 140 characters or less.

Building a successful AP career is simple common sense. It's not hard, but you need to do it right.

You need to focus on the following eight areas.

- Clarify the purpose and direction for your AP career.
- Commit to taking personal responsibility for your AP career.
- Build unshakeable self confidence.
- Create positive personal impact.
- Become an outstanding performer.
- Become a dynamic communicator.
- Build strong, lasting relationships.
- Take care of yourself.

The tweets that follow are divided into these eight categories.

They will show you how to put these eight concepts to work — and create the successful AP career you want and deserve.

Will tweet books replace traditional books? Probably not. But this little book will get you started creating a successful AP career.

Enjoy this book. But remember, I want to talk with you, not to you. Please tweet what you think about my ideas. @BudBilanich.

Each of the points I've made above is less than 140 characters.

See? You can communicate a lot of useful information in 140 characters or less. Enjoy the following tweets.

Clarity

CLARITY

1

Be proud of being an AP. You create successful days, successful meetings, successful conferences and successful businesses.

CLARITY

2

Define exactly what AP career success means to you. It's easier to hit a clear, unambiguous target.

CLARITY

3

The more clear you are about what success means to you personally, the easier it will be to create the successful AP career you want.

CLARITY

4

Emerson says, "Good luck is another name for tenacity of purpose." Pursue your purpose as an AP tenaciously.

CLARITY

5

Create a vivid mental image of yourself as a successful AP. This vivid image will keep you motivated when things get tough.

CLARITY

6

Visualization is powerful. The more vivid an image you have of you as an AP success, the more likely you are to achieve that success.

CLARITY

7

Your vivid mental image is a blueprint, a plan for your AP success, but you still have to do the work to make it a reality.

CLARITY

8

Visualize the euphoria of a successful AP career, not the pain of failure.

CLARITY

9

Use affirmations to create your vision of being a successful AP. Affirmations are the future stated in the present tense.

CLARITY

10

Clarify your personal values. Your values are your anchor. They are your guides to decision making in ambiguous situations.

CLARITY

11

Your personal values are things that you hold near and dear; things on which you absolutely will not compromise.

CLARITY

12

Your values come from deep inside you. Spend the time necessary to discover them. Then, hold fast to them; honor them by your actions.

CLARITY

13

Not every job can, or should, last forever.
Know when it's time to leave.

CLARITY

14

Recognize when your needs are no longer being met. But carefully evaluate your motives and goals before making career — and life — altering decisions.

CLARITY

15

Consider a job change if you feel that your work and your life no longer support one another.

Commitment

COMMITMENT

16

You're in charge! Commit to taking personal responsibility for creating the successful AP career you want and deserve.

COMMITMENT

17

Set and achieve S.M.A.R.T. goals for your AP career. S.M.A.R.T. goals are Specific, Measurable, Achievable, Relevant and Time Bound.

COMMITMENT

18

Goals are important for your successful AP career. You can't get where you want if you don't know where you're going.

COMMITMENT

19

Focus on your AP success goals several times a day. Spend your valuable time only on the things that will help you achieve them.

COMMITMENT

20

List the reasons for each goal you set for your AP success. These reasons will come in handy when you get tired and frustrated.

COMMITMENT

21

Keep your goals with you — in your wallet or on your screen saver. They will be a constant reminder to you of what you will achieve.

COMMITMENT

22

Write your goals. Share them with others. You are more likely to achieve goals that you write and share.

COMMITMENT

23

Aim high. Set and achieve high goals —
month after month and year after year
after year. Do whatever it takes to achieve
those goals.

COMMITMENT

24

Success is a journey, not a destination. When you accomplish one goal reach even higher and set a new one.

COMMITMENT

25

Stuff happens as you go about creating a successful AP career. Choose to respond positively to the negative stuff that happens.

COMMITMENT

26

Take personal responsibility for your success as an AP. No one is going to do it for you. Adopt the motto, "If it's to be, it's up to me."

COMMITMENT

27

Treat failures as the tuition you pay to succeed as an AP. When you have a setback, choose to react positively and learn something.

COMMITMENT

28

Persistent people keep going; especially in the face of difficulties. Keep at it to reach your goals and become a successful AP.

COMMITMENT

29

Don't be afraid to fail. You fail only if you don't learn something from the experience. Treat every failure as an opportunity to grow.

COMMITMENT

30

It's not what happens to you, but how you react to it. Don't dwell on the negative, use it as a springboard to action and creativity.

COMMITMENT

31

Don't let a slow day get you down. If you come back empty handed in your quest for AP success, get up the next day and keep working.

COMMITMENT

32

While other people and events have an impact on your life, they don't shape it. You get to choose how you react to people and events.

COMMITMENT

33

Vision without action is a daydream. No matter how big your plans and dreams, they'll never become a reality until you act on them.

COMMITMENT

34

Take responsibility for your mistakes. Accept feedback courteously and suggest possible solutions.

COMMITMENT

35

Blame is frustrating and a waste of time. Don't blame. Work with your colleagues to find solutions.

COMMITMENT

36

Demonstrate your commitment to taking personal responsibility for your AP career success. Be accountable for your work.

Confidence

CONFIDENCE

37

Self confidence must come from within. Outside reinforcement and strokes can help, but you have to build your own confidence.

CONFIDENCE

38

Focus on what you are becoming — a successful AP. This makes it easier to believe in yourself and is important to your AP success.

CONFIDENCE

39

Choose optimism. It builds your confidence. Believe that today will be better than yesterday and that tomorrow will be better yet.

CONFIDENCE

40

Optimism is contagious. Become a positive, optimistic person. Surround yourself with positive people. They will build your confidence.

CONFIDENCE

41

Be an optimist. Believe things will turn out well. When they don't, don't sulk. Learn what you can, use it the next time.

CONFIDENCE

42

Everyone is afraid sometime. Self confident people face their fears and act. Look your fears in the eye and do something.

CONFIDENCE

43

4 steps for dealing with fear that can sabotage your success. Identify it. Admit it. Accept it. Do something about it.

CONFIDENCE

44

Act. Feel the fear, and do it anyway. That's the definition of courage, and a great way to build your self confidence and AP success.

CONFIDENCE

45

Procrastination is the physical manifestation of fear and is a confidence killer. Act — especially when you're afraid.

CONFIDENCE

46

Surround yourself with positive people. Hold them close. They will give you energy and help you create the AP success you deserve.

CONFIDENCE

47

Jettison the negative people in your life. They are energy black holes. They will suck you dry; but only if you let them.

CONFIDENCE

48

Find a mentor, someone who will help you find the lessons in your setbacks and use them to move forward in your AP career.

CONFIDENCE

49

Identify the self confident people you know. Pay attention to how they act and carry themselves. Watch what they do. Act like them.

CONFIDENCE

50

Act as if you expect to be accepted, and you will be. This will increase your confidence and help you make a strong personal impact.

CONFIDENCE

51

Fake it till you make it. Appear to be self-confident and others will treat you as if you are. In turn, this will boost your confidence.

CONFIDENCE

52

Stand or sit up straight. Don't slouch.
Your mother was right. Good posture is
important. It makes you look self
confident.

CONFIDENCE

53

Think only of the best, work only for the best and expect only the best. Forget the mistakes of the past. Press on to better things.

CONFIDENCE

54

Be as enthusiastic about the success of others as you are about your own. Help all the people around recognize that they are special.

CONFIDENCE

55

Give so much time to building your self confidence and improving yourself that you have no time to criticize others.

CONFIDENCE

56

Take stock of yourself. What are your strengths? What are your weaknesses? Confident people emphasize their strengths.

Positive Personal Impact

POSITIVE PERSONAL IMPACT

57

Conduct yourself in a confident and professional manner. This will let others know that you respect and value your AP career choice.

POSITIVE PERSONAL IMPACT

58

Create and nurture your unique AP personal brand. Stand, and be known for, something. Make sure that everything you do is on brand.

POSITIVE PERSONAL IMPACT

59

Your personal brand should be unique to you, but built on integrity. Integrity is doing the right thing even when no one's looking.

POSITIVE PERSONAL IMPACT

60

Build your personal brand. Do whatever it takes to make sure that people will think of and remember you in the way you want them to.

POSITIVE PERSONAL IMPACT

61

Be visible. Volunteer for tough jobs.
Brand yourself as a person who can and
does make significant contributions.

POSITIVE PERSONAL IMPACT

62

Nurture your network. What your friends, colleagues, clients, and customers say about you is how others will think of your brand.

POSITIVE PERSONAL IMPACT

63

Demonstrate self respect. Be impeccable in your presentation of self — in person and on line.

POSITIVE PERSONAL IMPACT

64

Be well groomed and appropriate for every situation. Always dress one level up from what is expected. You'll stand out from the crowd.

POSITIVE PERSONAL IMPACT

65

"Business" is the first and most important word in "business casual." Dress like you're going to work, not a sporting event or club.

POSITIVE PERSONAL IMPACT

66

Observe successful APs in your organization. What do they wear? Dress like them and you won't go wrong.

POSITIVE PERSONAL IMPACT

67

21st Century technology has created new etiquette rules. Learn and use them to appear polished when you're on line.

POSITIVE PERSONAL IMPACT

68

Be gracious. Know and follow the basic rules of etiquette. Everybody likes to be around polite and mannerly people.

POSITIVE PERSONAL IMPACT

69

When someone compliments you, just say "thank you." When someone criticizes you, say "thank you, I'll work on that."

70

Learn and use simple table manners.
Good table manners make you look
polished and poised.

SUCCESS TWEETS FOR ADMINISTRATIVE PROFESSIONALS

71

Always act like a lady or gentleman. It's not old fashioned; it's smart business and leads to a successful AP career.

POSITIVE PERSONAL IMPACT

72

Keep your breath fresh. Brush after meals and coffee. Use the strips. Don't chew gum. Ever. It makes you look like a cow.

POSITIVE PERSONAL IMPACT

73

Say "thank you" often. You'll succeed in your AP career, build a strong personal brand and leave a legacy of being a nice person.

74

Be courteous. It costs you nothing, and it can mean everything to someone else. It also helps in getting what you want.

POSITIVE PERSONAL IMPACT

75

Learn and use the basic rules of etiquette. Social faux pas might not ruin your career, but they certainly won't help it.

POSITIVE PERSONAL IMPACT

76

Never spread a rumor. "Gossip" is not a good adjective to have attached to your name.

POSITIVE PERSONAL IMPACT

77

If you can't change a situation, or are unwilling to discuss it with someone who can, keep your opinions to yourself.

SUCCESS TWEETS FOR ADMINISTRATIVE PROFESSIONALS

POSITIVE PERSONAL IMPACT

78

Be courteous. Treat every colleague and visitor to the office as you would treat a guest in your own home.

POSITIVE PERSONAL IMPACT

79

Use correct grammar in your speech and in your correspondence. "Yeah" is not a word in the vocabulary of successful APs.

Outstanding Performance

OUTSTANDING PERFORMANCE

80

Become a lifelong learner. The half-life of knowledge is rapidly diminishing. Staying in the same place is the same as going backwards.

OUTSTANDING PERFORMANCE

81

Learn as fast, or faster, than the world changes. In a world that never stops changing, you can never stop learning and growing.

OUTSTANDING PERFORMANCE

82

Keep learning. Don't have your college degree? — get it. Always wanted to write poetry? — do it. Bring all of you to your work.

OUTSTANDING PERFORMANCE

83

You're never at the "top of your game." You're either improving or slowly becoming irrelevant. Keep improving.

OUTSTANDING PERFORMANCE

84

Master the technical disciplines associated with being an AP. Share what you know. Become the go to AP in your company.

OUTSTANDING PERFORMANCE

85

Attend every seminar and software class you can. Look for the one nugget that makes your job easier and enhances your AP career success.

OUTSTANDING PERFORMANCE

86

Stay up to date on your industry. Read industry publications. Know the hot topics for your company, competitors and industry.

OUTSTANDING PERFORMANCE

87

Choose personal discipline and you will never have to worry about external discipline.

OUTSTANDING PERFORMANCE

88

Always be on the lookout for new ideas. Find opportunities where others see obstacles. See the world through your own creative eyes.

OUTSTANDING PERFORMANCE

89

Positive time management is an important habit to develop. Habits are like muscles. The more you use them, the stronger they get.

OUTSTANDING PERFORMANCE

90

Determine your peak energy times. Schedule "high brain" tasks then and "low brain" tasks at times when your energy is lowest.

OUTSTANDING PERFORMANCE

91

Stay focused. Don't get distracted. Treat time as the precious commodity that it is. Manage your time and life well.

OUTSTANDING PERFORMANCE

92

Break large projects into smaller chunks.
They are not so overwhelming that way.
Set mini milestones for yourself.

OUTSTANDING PERFORMANCE

93

Get organized. Organize your time, life and workspace. Sweat the small stuff. Success is in execution. Execution is in the details.

OUTSTANDING PERFORMANCE

94

Create a unique AP personal organization system based on your needs and preferences and what works for you.

OUTSTANDING PERFORMANCE

95

The better you feel, the better your AP performance. Live a healthy lifestyle. Eat well. Exercise regularly. Get regular checkups.

OUTSTANDING PERFORMANCE

96

Get into a high performance mindset. Don't question yourself. Trust your AP skills and abilities. Do what you know how to do.

OUTSTANDING PERFORMANCE

97

Good truly is the enemy of great. Don't settle for good performance. Today, good is mediocre. Become a great performer.

OUTSTANDING PERFORMANCE

98

Don't worry about getting credit for doing the job. Worry about getting the job done well — accurately and on time.

OUTSTANDING PERFORMANCE

99

Get the job done with what you've got. Don't worry about what you don't have or would like to have.

OUTSTANDING PERFORMANCE

100

Care about what you do as an AP. If you care a little, you'll be an OK performer. If you care a lot, you'll become an outstanding AP.

OUTSTANDING PERFORMANCE

101

Expect delays. They always happen. Give yourself plenty of time to perform at your best.

OUTSTANDING PERFORMANCE

102

It's your job to find solutions to problems. Approach every challenge as an opportunity to develop your problem-solving skills.

OUTSTANDING PERFORMANCE

103

Perfection is counterproductive, stressful and overrated. Don't succumb to it. Cut yourself some slack.

OUTSTANDING PERFORMANCE

104

Extraordinary effort is not always rewarded by others. Enjoy the internal satisfaction of doing an outstanding job.

OUTSTANDING PERFORMANCE

105

Accept a helping hand. Don't be too proud, afraid or ashamed to ask for help or assistance from others.

OUTSTANDING PERFORMANCE

106

Each day, experience your own edge — the furthest place you can go. And each day, try to push past yesterday's edge.

OUTSTANDING PERFORMANCE

107

Let your performance speak for you. Never use your life circumstances to justify your request for a pay raise.

OUTSTANDING PERFORMANCE

108

Respect your work, yourself and others by giving your full attention to the task at hand.

OUTSTANDING PERFORMANCE

109

Never say you can't do something. Any solution in an application is just a click away on "Help."

OUTSTANDING PERFORMANCE

110

Keep your contact list up to date. Note not only personnel and phone number changes but promotions, titles, and company names.

OUTSTANDING PERFORMANCE

111

Archive, delete and begin new hard copy files at the beginning of a new year — follow company policy on retention and deletion of files.

OUTSTANDING PERFORMANCE

112

Keep your files clean. You don't need six copies of a draft when a final presentation is already done.

OUTSTANDING PERFORMANCE

113

Look at an email once and do something with it — reply to it, forward it, save it or delete it.

OUTSTANDING PERFORMANCE

114

Use on-line assistance such as http://
www.microsoft.com/atwork. They provide
assistance with all Microsoft products.

Dynamic Communication

DYNAMIC COMMUNICATION

115

All dynamic communicators have mastered three basic communication skills: conversation, writing and presenting.

DYNAMIC COMMUNICATION

116

We're all in sales. You have to sell yourself every day. You need to become an excellent communicator to sell your ideas.

SUCCESS TWEETS FOR ADMINISTRATIVE PROFESSIONALS

117

To become a dynamic communicator,
speak from your heart. Show that you
care — about yourself and the people
with whom you are speaking.

DYNAMIC COMMUNICATION

118

Learn how to handle yourself in conversation. A brief conversation with the right person can greatly help — or hinder — your AP career.

DYNAMIC COMMUNICATION

119

Conversation tips: be warm, pleasant and gracious and sensitive to the interpersonal needs and anxieties of others.

DYNAMIC COMMUNICATION

120

Demonstrate your understanding of others' points of view. Listen well and ask questions if you don't understand.

DYNAMIC COMMUNICATION

121

There is no one-size-fits-all approach to conversation success. What you say is often less important than how you say it.

DYNAMIC COMMUNICATION

122

Simplify your message. Know what you want to say and what you want others to do. Don't let your true meaning get lost in the clutter.

DYNAMIC COMMUNICATION

123

Listen more than you speak. Pay attention to what other people say; respond appropriately.

124

Live people take precedence over phone calls. Continue in person conversations, rather than answering your cell phone.

125

Use the 2/3 – 1/3 rule. Listen two thirds
of the time; speak one third of the time.
Focus your complete attention on the
other person.

DYNAMIC COMMUNICATION

126

Remember and use people's names. Look for common ground with the people you meet. Find out about them, their hobbies and passions.

DYNAMIC COMMUNICATION

127

Become a clear, concise writer. Make your writing easy to read and easy to understand. Use simple straightforward language.

DYNAMIC COMMUNICATION

128

Write clearly and simply: short words and sentences; first person; active voice. Be precise in your choice of words.

DYNAMIC COMMUNICATION

129

Use the active voice in your writing. Say "I suggest we do this," rather than "It is suggested that…"

DYNAMIC COMMUNICATION

130

Always proofread your work. Spell check will catch misspellings but cannot point out if you've used an incorrect word.

DYNAMIC COMMUNICATION

131

Proofread because you might have forgotten an important point or typed in a wrong number.

DYNAMIC COMMUNICATION

132

Become an excellent presenter.
Presentations are important. Careers
have been made on the strength of one or
two good presentations.

DYNAMIC COMMUNICATION

133

Presentations are opportunities to shine. Don't let stage fright rob you of your opportunity. Get control of your nerves.

DYNAMIC COMMUNICATION

134

Presentation steps: 1) Determine the message. 2) Analyze the audience. 3) Organize the information. 4) Design visuals. 5) Practice.

DYNAMIC COMMUNICATION

135

Presentations are easy to create. Write your closing first, your opening next. Then fill in the content. Practice, practice, practice.

DYNAMIC COMMUNICATION

136

Discipline yourself to prepare for presentations. Practice out loud until you are totally in sync with what you're going to say.

Relationship
Building

RELATIONSHIP BUILDING

137

Use every social interaction to build and strengthen relationships. Strong relationships are your ticket to a successful AP career.

RELATIONSHIP BUILDING

138

Relationships are two-way streets. They are never the sole responsibility of just one person.

RELATIONSHIP BUILDING

139

Get genuinely interested in others. Help bring out the best in everyone you know. Others will gravitate to you.

RELATIONSHIP BUILDING

140

Keep confidences. Don't embarrass others by repeating what they share with you — even if it isn't in confidence.

RELATIONSHIP BUILDING

141

Everyone has something to offer. Never dismiss anyone out of hand. Take the initiative. Actively build relationships with others.

RELATIONSHIP BUILDING

142

Get to know yourself. Use your self knowledge to better understand others and build mutually beneficial relationships with them.

RELATIONSHIP BUILDING

143

Every person is unique. AP career success comes from honoring the uniqueness of every person must you meet.

RELATIONSHIP BUILDING

144

Know and accept yourself to find inner harmony. Know and accept others to create harmonious AP working relationships.

RELATIONSHIP BUILDING

145

Pay it forward. Build relationships by giving with no expectation of return. Give of yourself and time to build strong relationships.

RELATIONSHIP BUILDING

146

When meeting someone new ask yourself, "What can I do to help this person?" By thinking this first, you'll build stronger relationships.

RELATIONSHIP BUILDING

147

There is no quid pro quo in effective relationships. Do for others without being asked or waiting for them to do for you.

RELATIONSHIP BUILDING

148

Be generous. By giving with no expectation of return, you'll be surprised by how much comes back to you in the long run.

RELATIONSHIP BUILDING

149

Be helpful whenever you can without expecting to get help in return. It is more likely you will get help when you give it.

RELATIONSHIP BUILDING

150

Help not to get help but to build relationships and show you are a team player.

RELATIONSHIP BUILDING

151

Be happy to see others succeed.
Successful APs use the success of others
to motivate themselves to greater success.

RELATIONSHIP BUILDING

152

Trust is the glue that holds relationships together. The more you demonstrate trust in others, the more they will trust you.

RELATIONSHIP BUILDING

153

Resolve conflict positively. Treat conflict as an opportunity to strengthen, not destroy, the AP relationships you've worked hard to build.

RELATIONSHIP BUILDING

154

Be a consensus builder. Focus on where you agree with other people. It will be easier to resolve differences and create agreement.

RELATIONSHIP BUILDING

155

Respect means resolving differences and problems in a productive way that preserves the self-worth of the other person.

156

Influence with your personal power, don't intimidate. Intimidation is used to control people, not build relationships with them.

RELATIONSHIP BUILDING

157

Be responsible for yourself. No one can "make you angry." Choose to act in a civil, forthright, constructive manner in tense situations.

RELATIONSHIP BUILDING

158

Do your job; give credit to others for doing theirs. Everyone likes to work with people who share the credit for a job well done.

RELATIONSHIP BUILDING

159

We all make mistakes. Own up to yours. You'll become known as a straight shooter — honest with yourself and with others.

RELATIONSHIP BUILDING

160

Become a widely trusted AP. Deliver on what you say you'll do. If you can't meet a commitment, let the other person know right away.

RELATIONSHIP BUILDING

161

Honor your limits and others will do the same. Establish boundaries and protect them in a polite, professional yet assertive way.

RELATIONSHIP BUILDING

162

Make connections at seminars. Your expertise or theirs may come in handy when a challenging situation comes up.

RELATIONSHIP BUILDING

163

You may want to write a nasty email. Go ahead. Just don't send it! Think before doing something that can harm your AP career.

164

Always send a congratulatory email when you receive an email announcing that a colleague you have has been promoted or retired,

RELATIONSHIP BUILDING

165

Don't share personal information unless you're willing to have it "shouted from the rooftops."

Taking Care Of Yourself

TAKING CARE OF YOURSELF

166

Be kind to yourself. Accept yourself.
Love yourself and who you are.

167

Take care of yourself. Do what you need to do to feel good about yourself, your life and your AP career.

TAKING CARE OF YOURSELF

168

Choose to be you — don't wait for other people's permission to live your life and pursue your career success.

169

Play on the winning team. Be hopeful and abundant. Hope defeats fear. Abundance defeats scarcity.

TAKING CARE OF YOURSELF

170

You get what you expect. Expect the best in your AP career and you'll get it.

TAKING CARE OF YOURSELF

171

When you focus on what's going right in your life and AP career, things will begin going right more often.

TAKING CARE OF YOURSELF

172

Stand on your principles when you must.
Go with the flow most of the time.

TAKING CARE OF YOURSELF

173

Take time to appreciate the setbacks and defeats in your AP career. This will help you appreciate your victories even more.

TAKING CARE OF YOURSELF

174

Be peaceful. When you're at peace with yourself and the world, you're in a great place to build the AP career success you deserve.

TAKING CARE OF YOURSELF

175

It's difficult to be at peace with yourself when you are afraid of the consequences of your actions.

176

Blame, resentments and envy get in the way of taking care of yourself and creating the AP career success you deserve.

TAKING CARE OF YOURSELF

177

Forgiveness precedes peace and harmony. Forgive others. More important, forgive yourself.

TAKING CARE OF YOURSELF

178

Choose to align yourself with your circumstances. Be strong in the face of problems, setbacks and discord.

TAKING CARE OF YOURSELF

179

Get balanced. Nurture the needs of your mind, body, emotions and spirit.

TAKING CARE OF YOURSELF

180

Be yourself. Celebrate your uniqueness as a human being and as an AP.

TAKING CARE OF YOURSELF

181

Get out and visit the people and places that bring you joy and happiness. You deserve it.

TAKING CARE OF YOURSELF

182

When you wake up every morning, envision yourself as having a great day filled with success and happiness.

TAKING CARE OF YOURSELF

183

Every night before you go to sleep, think about the good things that happened to you that day. Sleep in appreciation of them.

TAKING CARE OF YOURSELF

184

Guilt is a feeling we let others project on us. Don't let guilt run your life or hurt your AP career success.

TAKING CARE OF YOURSELF

185

Listen, really listen, to your friends. Choose friends who will really listen to you.

TAKING CARE OF YOURSELF

186

Finish the unfinished stuff that preys on your mind — or let it go. You'll be happier and more successful.

TAKING CARE OF YOURSELF

187

Take time to appreciate the beauty in the world. You'll be happier and more at peace.

TAKING CARE OF YOURSELF

188

Take a walk, a long one. Open yourself up to your thoughts. Walking meditation is a great way to relax and recharge.

TAKING CARE OF YOURSELF

189

Get in touch with your feelings. They will guide you and keep you on the path to inner peace and AP career success.

TAKING CARE OF YOURSELF

190

Hit the minimize button on your inner critic. Use affirmations and positive self talk to guide your journey to AP career success.

TAKING CARE OF YOURSELF

191

Get involved with something outside of your AP work about which you are passionate. You'll be more balanced, happy and productive.

TAKING CARE OF YOURSELF

192

Find the common ground with those with whom you are in conflict. It's there. You just have to look for it.

TAKING CARE OF YOURSELF

193

Laugh. Laugh often. Laugh loud. It's good for the soul. Laughter will energize you and keep you going when things get tough.

TAKING CARE OF YOURSELF

194

Choose compassion. Others will respond in kind.

TAKING CARE OF YOURSELF

195

Giving in to your anger is easy. Don't do it. Choose forgiveness.

TAKING CARE OF YOURSELF

196

Happiness and peace begin with a smile. Smile and be happy and peaceful.

197

Put down your baggage. It's heavy and weighing you down. The road to AP career success is easier when you're traveling light.

TAKING CARE OF YOURSELF

198

Honor your history by learning from it. Then, put it in a box and put the box on a shelf in your mind.

TAKING CARE OF YOURSELF

199

No one ever became an AP career success without truly believing he or she deserved it. You get what you're willing to receive.

TAKING CARE OF YOURSELF

200

Your emotions can strengthen or weaken your spirit. Recognize the difference and act accordingly.

201

And, because I always over deliver,
here is one more very important tweet...

Knowing is not enough. Successful APs
will both read and act on this advice.
Take action. Be the successful AP I know
you can be.

About Bud Bilanich

Bud Bilanich, The Common Sense Guy, is a success coach, motivational speaker, author and blogger who helps his clients succeed by applying their common sense. He writes a popular career success blog five days a week that you can find at www.BudBilanich.com.

Dr. Bilanich is Harvard educated but has a no nonsense approach to his coaching speaking and writing that goes back to his roots in the steel country of Western Pennsylvania. His approach to life and career success is a result of over 35 years of business experience, 10 years of research and study of successful people and the application of common sense.

Bud is the author of 15 books on leadership and career and life success, including *Success Tweets, Straight Talk for Success, 42 Rules to Jumpstart Your Professional Success, Your Success GPS*.

His clients include Pfizer, Glaxo SmithKline, Merck, Johnson and Johnson, Abbot Laboratories, PepsiCo, AT&T, Chase Manhattan Bank,

Citigroup, General Motors, UBS, AXA Advisors, Cabot Corporation, The Aetna, PECO Energy, Olin Corporation, Minerals Technologies, The Boys and Girls Clubs of America and a number of small and family owned businesses.

Bud is a cancer survivor and lives in Denver Colorado with his wife Cathy. He is a retired rugby player and an avid cyclist. He likes movies, live theatre and crime fiction.

About Ketty Ortega

Ketty Ortega is an Administrative Professional with over 35 years of experience. Currently she is a Site Operations Assistant at a large multinational pharmaceutical company overseeing office administration and security.

Ketty has enjoyed a number career opportunities including SAT instructor, FLEX program Spanish teacher, Acquisition Assistant for a large multinational cosmetic company and executive assistant for a national accreditation office for the arts.

Ketty particularly enjoys her interaction with colleagues and finding creative ways of bringing colleagues together such as Soup Extravaganza Contests, Tacky Holiday Sweater Events and Food and Clothes Donation Drives. Ketty is also a student at heart and enjoys learning all the latest computer features which adds to her job proficiency.

Ketty lives in Reston with her husband, Robert. They have one child, Andria, who lives in NY.

In her spare time, Ketty enjoys writing poetry and short story fiction.

About Chrissy Scivicque

Chrissy Scivicque (pronounced "Civic") is an award-winning freelance writer and editor with a passion for two things: food and helping others. As a Certified Nutritionist and experienced career coach, she combined her two loves and built EatYourCareer.com, a website dedicated to helping others create the nourishing professional lives they deserve.

As a career coach, Chrissy helps people develop strategies and take meaningful action towards achieving career goals. Her philosophy encourages clients to take an active role in managing their career path and to do so with a holistic point-of-view in order to create a truly fulfilling professional experience.

Visit Chrissy at EatYourCareer.com and pick up a copy of her free mini-workbook, *"How Nourishing is Your Career?"*

Free Gifts For You

Now that you've read these 201 tweets on Administrative Professional success, you may want to read more about career success. That's why I've decided to give you a gift — several in fact.

Go to http://www.SuccessTweets.com/freegifts. When you register you will receive . . .

· *Straight Talk for Success*
· *Star Power: Common Sense Ideas for Career and Life Success*
· *I Want YOU...To Succeed*

I will also include the audio book version of *Straight Talk for Success,* and a set of digital mem-cards that highlight the information in *Straight Talk.*

Also, I will send you 25 of my best success tips in audio form. You'll get two a week for 12½ weeks.

Finally, you will begin receiving my daily success quotes.

I really want you to be able to create the life and career success that you want and deserve. That's why I wrote *Success Tweets,* and that's why I'm giving you these other gifts.

Just go to http://www.SuccessTweets.com/ freegifts/, enter your name and email address, and you'll be directed to a page where you can download all of the free gifts.

My final wish for you comes from my favorite recording artist, Bob Dylan. "May you build a ladder to the stars and climb on every rung." I hope your ladder takes you wherever you want to go in your Administrative Professional career.

Check me out on Twitter @BudBilanich.

Bud Bilanich
March 2011
Denver, CO USA

Success Tweets for Administrative Professional
makes a great gift!

Quantity discounts are available
from the publisher.

Call 303.393.0446 to inquire
about quantity pricing.